CHARLES DE FOUCAULD

dedicated to the memory
of the author,
J. Frawley 1930-99

*All booklets are published thanks to the
generous support of the members of the
Catholic Truth Society*

CATHOLIC TRUTH SOCIETY
PUBLISHERS TO THE HOLY SEE

CONTENTS

Introduction 3
Early Life 4
    Adolescence 6
    The Soldier 7
    The Explorer 10
    Failed love 12
Conversion 14
    The Trappist 16
    In the Holy Land 19
Algeria: Beni Abbés 25
    Deeper in the desert 28
    Brother Michel 32
    The Tuareg Dictionary 36
    Charles' idea for an order 37
    Return to Tamanrasset 38
    World War: the fort at Tamanrasset 40
Some Writings of Brother Charles 45
    For the sake of Jesus and the Gospel 45
    The young agnostic 45
    Vocation: 'as Jesus of Nazareth' 46
    Your Rule 47
    Poor like Jesus 48
    Your way of praying 49
    Your relationship with others 50
    'All things to all people' 52
    Preparing for death 52
The Legacy of Brother Charles 55
    The Little Brothers 55
    The Little Sisters 56
To Contact for Further Information 60

INTRODUCTION

Soldier, playboy, explorer, Trappist monk, and the inspiration behind a new current of spirituality, Charles de Foucauld's life has fascinated many Christians of the twentieth century. Having left his Trappist monastery to be closer to 'ordinary' poor people, Charles both symbolically, and in fact, inaugurated a new way of Christian and religious life which left behind the strict separations of the cloister, or the convent walls, and aimed at a more natural, less institutionalised way of being Church. This way which Charles called, 'Nazareth', wanted to imitate as closely as possible the hidden life Jesus had lived as a poor carpenter at Nazareth. Although he did not succeed in founding the religious congregations he dreamed of in his own lifetime, Br. Charles' ideals have proved to be well ahead of his time.

EARLY LIFE

Charles de Foucauld was born at Strasbourg in France on September 15th, 1858. When he was a year old his father was appointed Chief Inspector of Woods and Forests and the family moved thirty miles northward to Wissembourg.

The first few years must have been happy. He and his younger sister had loving parents. But very soon things began to go wrong. His father, whose health had been causing concern, moved to his sister's residence in Paris. His malady has been variously described as tuberculosis and depression. Then came a disaster involving their mother Elizabeth. She died suddenly, probably as a result of a miscarriage. Five months later her husband died. The cocoon of love and security, which had surrounded the two children, was thus rudely shattered.

Charles and his sister, Mimi, were brought to the Strasbourg home of Colonel De Morlet, their maternal grandfather. Two years later Charles wrote happy letters to his cousin Adolph, a young naval officer. He spoke of his liking for bacon and chocolate cake. His more than healthy appetite was already attracting attention. At a children's party he was seen gobbling up the cakes before the others had a chance to join in the feast.

Charles' schooling was disrupted by events outside his grandfather's control. At the age of eight the boy was enrolled in the diocesan school of Saint Arbrogast. He spent eighteen months there until the school closed in 1868. He next went to the Imperial Lycée at Strasbourg. He was a conscientious and energetic pupil and it was noted there that he was particularly good at Latin.

During the war between France and Prussia the family had to leave Strasbourg, which was right on the border and spend some months at Berne and Interlaken in Switzerland. Then they returned to France and settled at Nancy. Alsace was now German territory and Nancy was as near to the disputed province as the Colonel could get while remaining in France.

Charles entered the Lycée National of Nancy in 1871. He was later to speak of the lack of religious formation which was a feature of the Lycée regime. "Young people need to be taught," he wrote, "by people of genuine holiness and real depth of conviction... They need teachers who know their faith, and can give reasons for what they believe, and who can inspire young people with confidence in the truth of their faith".

It was in the Cathedral of Nancy that Charles received his first Holy Communion in 1872. Charles' cousin Marie de Moitessier came from Paris for the ceremony. She brought as a present a book which Charles did not read for many years but which he treasured and which was later to influence his religious thinking. It was Bossuet's 'Elevations sur les Mysteres'.

Adolescence

Eight years older than Charles, Marie became his trusted
friend and confidante, She spoke to him of the love of the
Sacred Heart of Jesus and this love was to become, after his
conversion, the inspiration for Charles' unique and heroic
service. Marie's marriage to Vicomte Olivier de Bondy was
a traumatic experience for the boy, now a teenager.

Around the age of 15, Charles began to lose his childhood faith. Intelligent and an avid reader, he plunged on
his own initiative into the works of the intellectual scep-
tics then in vogue: Voltaire, Montaigne, Littré. He was
unable, as he later complained, to find 'a reasoned
account of Christian beliefs'. And he was shocked to dis-
cover the wide variety of conflicting religions: "the equal
faith with which different religions were held", he wrote
later to a friend who was having doubts, "appeared as the
condemnation of them all". For "nothing can be proved
about God" and "truth cannot be found": "I despaired of
truth", he was to say, "particularly of the truths of God's
trinitarian being and incarnation." The 'loss' of his cousin
Marie, his 'second mother' and 'confidante' - due to her
marriage and hence 'distance' from him and his concerns
- and soon after, the death of his dearly loved grandfather,
disturbed him deeply. This intellectual and affectionate
'void', as he later described it, provided the background
to his loss of faith, or rather his inability to allow God to
convert his childhood piety into an authentic adult faith.

And having lost his faith and with it any positive motivation, he turned to a life of careless idleness and later of profligate extravagance.

1874 was also the year in which Charles was admitted as a boarder to the Jesuit school in the Rue des Postes in Paris. He was withdrawn from the college less than two years later. Charles had shown himself to be an uncooperative student, more interested in the girls who worked in the shops he frequented than he was in his studies. Due to his reading of sceptical literature, he had already lost his faith. He was later to describe his frame of mind thus: "At seventeen I was all egoism, all impiety, all desire for evil, I was as one bewitched."

The Soldier

It was decided that Charles should have a tutor to help him to prepare for admission to the military academy of St. Cyr. He became a student of the academy in October 1876. He carried too much weight to cut a sprightly figure in uniform. Among the students of the college who came closer to the military ideal were Henri Lapperine, with whom he formed an abiding friendship, and Henri Philippe Petain who was to become the hero of Verdun, and Marshal of France but who was, sadly, to die in disgrace on the Ile d'Yeu in 1945.

Only half of the eight hundred students were practicing Catholics. Charles belonged to the ranks of the unbelievers. Perhaps it was to compensate for loss of faith that he occasionally dipped into the Latin and Greek authors, especially Aristophanes. He neglected his studies and trusted his lucky star to get him through his examinations. But he did enough to earn himself a pass mark and qualified for entry into the Cavalry College at Saumur.

In the meantime Colonel de Morlet had died. The death of his grandfather meant the loss of the benign restraining influence he had exercised over Charles. During his stay in Saumur the young soldier frequented the most expensive restaurants eating and drinking to his heart's content. He had a special preference for partridge and venison followed by a dish of grated sweet chestnut topped with icecream. He also cast aside the old carelessness which had characterised his dress at Saint Cyr. He now patronised the most fashionable tailors and boot makers. Perhaps his new found fastidiousness was linked to another habit he had developed, the acquisition of mistresses.

But this wild living did not fulfill the deeper longings of his heart. His restlessness showed up in a number of strange escapades. On one of these occasions he went missing and, when the police were alerted, they found him wandering in the countryside disguised as a beggar.

Charles passed his final examination at Saumur, distinguishing himself by occupying eighty seventh place in a class of eighty seven. Now a 'finished' cavalry officer he spent some time at Cézanne and then at Pont-a-Mousson near Nancy. At Nancy he acquired a mistress whom he loved deeply and to whom he surprisingly gave the nickname 'Mimi', his sister's name. To please Mimi, Charles gave wild, expensive parties.

Serious living, however, had to continue and Charles' regiment, the Fourth Chasseurs d'Afrique, was ordered to French North Africa. Charles sent Mimi ahead of him to Africa, passing her off as 'Vicomtesse de Foucauld'. On her voyage to the port of Bone she had her meals at the captain's table. However, the disguise eventually proved transparent. Charles, who had now joined his regiment in Africa, was called to the office of the colonel. The latter felt that Charles' conduct in passing his mistress off as his wife was an insult to the officer class. But the young officer chose to leave the regiment rather than send Mimi home. He left North Africa and settled with Mimi at Evian.

But Africa and the army had made a deep impression on the apparently restless young man. The Fourth Chasseurs were called into active service and Charles felt that he should answer the call. He left Mimi in France and she disappeared from his life forever.

He and his fellow officer Lapperine, with whom he had formed an abiding friendship, believed that the French had an almost divine right to rule as much of Africa as they could acquire by treaty or conquest. Lapperine was destined to achieve military glory by reason of his dedication to the French cause. Charles wrote of him: "Lapperine gave the Sahara to France in spite of herself and united our possessions in Algeria with our Sudanese colonies".

The Explorer

Charles' military career was then disrupted by another dream. This time he felt the urge to explore part of Morocco, though this bright idea did not impress his family. He was being true, they felt, to his unpredictable self and seemed destined for anything rather than the military honours they wished for him. His Aunt Ines went so far as insisting that the finances of the soldier turned explorer should be managed by another member of the family, a cousin to Charles.

Before travelling to Morocco, Charles embarked on a period of intensive study as preparation for the demanding field work which lay ahead of him. He was encouraged and assisted by a librarian named McCarthy. McCarthy was the son of a Cork man who had joined the army of Napoleon. He had been an explorer and only turned to library work when his dream of travelling to Timbuktu had been abandoned. He was generous enough to do all he could to help this young Frenchman who had an opportunity of surpassing his own dreams of exploration and glory.

In Morocco a Jewish Rabbi named Mardochee was selected as a guide for Charles and he posed as

Mardochee's son. There was a scattering of people of Jewish race in Algeria and Morocco. Consequently, the disguise would make it easier for him to pass unnoticed and to find accommodation and provisions.

During the year or so which the pair spent in Morocco, Charles mapped seven hundred square miles which had never previously been mapped. He loved Morocco and this affection made the writing of the journal of his expedition an agreeable task for him. He wrote lyrically of the oases:

"There are varied trees, but palm trees more than any others; under their shade the ground, divided into squares, disappears under maize and millet, grass and vegetables. A multitude of canals water these rich plantations; here and there great basins are filled to the brim with water. This luxuriant vegetation, these superb trees which cast a thick shade on a completely green earth, those thousand canals, that admirable sky, those rich and laughing delights of nature, which, in the midst of a most desolate countryside, make dwelling here full of delights, all are found as well in other oases.... such are all those places where we see the date palm flourishing; in all of them the same freshness, the same calm, the same abundance; charming spots where it seems that only happy people could live."

Outside the oases the nomadic people might have been happy but they were not particularly virtuous: "The law of the strongest is alone respected. There are no quarrels

and bargains as with the oasis dwellers; on the contrary
thefts and murders are more frequent. You are only safe if
you place yourself under the protection and perpetual
care of a man, or a tribe... This is a temporary guarantee
of safety, created especially for travellers." Highway rob-
bery was common and Charles was robbed of everything
except his explorer's equipment and his precious notes.

Failed love

Shortly after his Moroccan expedition Charles went to
Algiers to consult with a professional geographer, a
Monsieur Titre. He fell in love with the geographer's
daughter. The young woman, born a Protestant had been
received into the Catholic Church. This should have facil-
itated marriage although Charles at the time did not have
any faith. The hoped for marriage, however, did not take
place. Charles succumbed to the snobbish opposition of
his own family. Mademoiselle Titre had no 'de' to her
name, being the daughter of a mere geographer without
aristocratic connections. Charles was to suffer for his
strange capitulation to the objections of his extended family. When he met the woman again a few years before his
death she told him she had abandoned her practice of the
faith because of his treatment of her. Charles, who was by
then a priest and a mystic, must have been profoundly
disturbed by the revelation. But his prayers for her were
answered and in 1927 Madame Doucet-Titre prefaced her

statement to the Postulator of Charles' cause with a prayer to Mary and the Holy Spirit and spoke in striking language of her admiration and affection for Charles.

She has left us a vivid description of Charles: "He had a very delicate skin, very lustrous, very white; also remarkable hair, eyes and a moustache that added great charm to his face. The general impression he made was one of alertness and he was most engaging. The fine velvety black eyes varied between infinite gentleness, untamed strength and tremendous will-power: sometimes his eyes sparkled in lively fashion. He talked very well, quietly, seriously or tenderly, ever in control of himself, never carried away, always deeply thoughtful, and without being cynical. Always perfectly groomed, never slovenly and always looking very much the officer."

CONVERSION

After an expedition to El Golea in Algeria in 1885, Charles returned to Paris to prepare his book on Morocco for publication. He had been awarded the Gold Medal of the Geographical Society and he could now, had he wished, become a person of distinction in Parisian society. But his sojourn in Algeria and Morocco had made him aware of a great void within his soul. "The sight of the Muslim faith", he said, "of these souls living in the continual presence of God, gave me a glimpse of something vaster and more real than worldly preoccupations".

With the help and encouragement of his cousin Marie de Bondy he began to drop into Churches to pray after his fashion to the God in whom he did not believe. His prayer was: "My God if you exist, make yourself known to me."

One of the churches he visited was the church of St. Augustin. The priest there, Abbé Huvelin, was celebrated for his preaching but still more for his saintliness and his sympathetic approach to human suffering and sin. It was said of him that his manner of saying Mass was his most beautiful method of preaching. One morning in October 1886 Charles went to the Church of St Augustin and stood at the grille of the Abbé's confessional. He told the priest simply that he did not have the Faith. The Abbé replied: "Kneel down and make your confession to God, you will believe".

"But I did not come for that".

"Make your confession!"

After the absolution the Abbé told him that since he was fasting he should receive Communion. And so Charles made his second First Communion, his holy confession having erased his years of unbelief and sin. The Abbé advised Charles to go to Mass and Holy Communion every day and several times a week he received the penitent at his house.

His cousin Marie again spoke to Charles of the love of the Sacred Heart of Jesus. Charles began to think seriously about a life "lived for God alone", through imitating Jesus as closely as possible. "Our Lord", said the Abbé "took the last place so thoroughly that no one has ever been able to take it away from Him". Charles spent the remainder of his life trying to rob his Divine Master of 'the last place'.

In 1888 Charles' book *"Reconnaissance Au Maroc"* (Exploration of Morocco) was published.

Perhaps it was his routine of daily prayer and solitary walks which convinced his cousin Marie that Charles should join the Cistercians. When she took him on a visit to the Abbey of Fontgombault he noticed that the lay brother who entertained Marie's children wore a very ragged habit. This impressed Charles. He wanted to imitate the monk's poverty. But he was called back to serve in the army for a short spell. This time he impressed the senior officers with his attention to his duties and his natural ability to command and lead.

His spell in the army over, Charles was advised by the Abbé Huvelin to make a pilgrimage to the Holy Land. When Charles reached Nazareth he was deeply impressed by experiencing the surroundings of so much of the Master's life. When he got back to France he spoke of his desire "to keep silent, to kneel at God's feet and to gaze at Him almost in silence". He applied for admission to the Cistercian Monastery of Our Lady of the Snows.

The Trappist

In December 1889 he said goodbye to his sister and her husband. In January he said goodbye to his cousin Marie. He said later "It was a sacrifice which cost me all my tears". In the same month he journeyed to Our Lady of the Snows in the bleak wind-swept Ardeche.

Charles now became Brother Marie Alberic and began the Cistercian routine of early rising, Divine Office, Mass, private prayer and manual labour with a few sparse meals consisting mainly of bread, cheese, and vegetables. It was an excellent way of life for someone whose dearest wish was to keep Our Lord company in His sufferings. But Charles had arranged before his entry into Our Lady of the Snows that, after six months of probation, he would be transferred to a poorer monastery in Syria.

If life in Our Lady of the Snows had been penitential, life in the Syrian monastery at Akbès was doubly so. There was a stone church but the rest of the abbey consisted of wattle huts with thatched roofs. The daily workload was extremely demanding. Charles carried stones, gathered cotton and hewed wood. He helped with the laundry and picked grapes. When his feet became swollen he was promoted to the offices of librarian and bell-ringer. He did not complain at the burden of his daily tasks but he found obedience difficult. He was also uneasy at times at the 'ease' and security of the monk's way of life which, despite its rigour, did not equal the poverty of the peasants in the surrounding countryside.

One day, Charles had to leave the monastery to visit the family of a Christian Syrian who was dying of cholera. Charles was struck by the contrast between the relative comfort of his monastery and the conditions of the poor. Mitigations to the Cistercian rule made at about that time did not please Charles. He began to dream of two new congregations of men and women who would follow Our Lord's life more to the rule: stricter poverty; much prayer but not in choir; communal life in smaller groups, without a hierarchy - everyone was to be a brother and sister of Jesus.

However, Charles continued in the Trappist order. After having pronounced his first vows in 1892, he began to study theology, a subject for which he did not have unqualified admiration. "Did St. Joseph know any?" he asked.

1896 was a distressing year for him. That was the year of the Armenian massacres. Christians suffered at the hands of Imperial Turkey. At Marache, a town near the monastery of Akbès, four thousand people died. Charles was unhappy because he knew that the immunity of the monks was due to their being European. He wrote: "The Europeans are protected by the Turkish government... It is very painful to stand in the good graces of those who slaughter our brothers... It is a disgrace to all Europe; with a single word she could have prevented these horrors."

He regretted the fact that he was not a priest. He would have liked to have gone out among the Christians, ministering to them and encouraging them to die for God.

But his vocation to the priesthood was not a matter which he took for granted. It would have placed him above ordinary people: whereas he sought the last place. Later he wrote that a sentence of the Abbé Huvelin had made a great impact on him: 'Jesus so took the last place that no one since has ever been able to take it from him.' If Charles was ordained a priest, wouldn't he forfeit that treasured last place?

Throughout his time as a Trappist, Charles continued his correspondence with Abbé Huvelin. At first, the Abbé encouraged Charles to continue as a Trappist. So Charles went, at his abbott's direction, to Staouëli near Algiers and from there to Rome to continue his study of philosophy and theology, which he now began to appreciate. However, he still longed for a life of poverty, prayer and service outside the monastic regime. Soon his superiors, recognising that he had a very special vocation, released him from his monastic vows.

In the Holy Land

Charles made private vows of chastity and poverty and travelled to the Holy Land on a ticket the Cistercians had bestowed on him. He went to Nazereth where he hoped to relive, in so far as that was possible, the life of Jesus the Worker. He was once more a pilgrim and an explorer. He was, in fact, taking another step on the road which was to lead to Tamanrasset. Charles reached Nazareth in March 1897. He was fortunate to get the kind of job he wanted. The Vicomte de Foucauld was installed at the convent of the Poor Clares as sacristan, postboy and jack of all trades. A toolshed fitted the dual role of workshop and living quarters. He could, and did, spend his free time in hour after hour of prayer before Jesus in the Blessed Sacrament. In one of his meditations, he imagined Jesus speaking to him (and to all people) about his life in Nazareth:

"After my presentation and my flight into Egypt, I withdrew to Nazareth. There I spent the years of my childhood and youth, until I was thirty years of age. Once again, it was for your sake I went there, for love of you. What was the meaning of that part of my life? I led it for your instruction. I instructed you continually for thirty years, not in words, but by silence and example. What was I teaching you? I was teaching you primarily that it is possible to do good to men - great good... divine good - without using words, without preaching, without fuss, but by silence and by giving them a good example."

Charles' love and concern for his family remained strong. When a baby of his sister's died, he wrote: "I have already prayed to him, that little saint, my nephew... pray to him always, my dear Marie."

The Poor Clares also had a convent near Jerusalem. The Abbess there expressed a wish to make the acquaintance of the French Vicomte who lived like a beggar. Charles agreed to be transferred to the Jerusalem convent.

Charles remained in Jerusalem for six months. He lived there the kind of life he had lived at Nazareth. From the window of the convent he could view all Jerusalem, the Mount of Olives and Bethany. From the other side of the building he could see the Cenacle, the path from there to the Garden of Gethsemane, Calvary, the dome of the Basilica of the Holy Sepulchre and the place of the Ascension.

Charles fulfilled the expectations of Abbess Elizabeth. He performed the tasks assigned to him with great humility. He spent any time he could spare from work and prayer painting pictures for the sisters. For neighbours he had an African couple who acted as caretakers for the convent. Charles referred to them as 'my brother and sister' and they referred to him as 'the gentleman'. Mother Elizabeth told her community that they had a saint living at their doorstep. Encouraged by Mother Elizabeth, Charles began to think again of the priesthood.

Towards ordination

The year 1900 was a turning point for Charles. He had a number of ideas concerning different projects, notably one to buy the Mount of Beatitudes, the small hill at the edge of the lake of Galilee where Jesus is supposed to have preached his 'Sermon on the Mount.' Charles' idea was to establish himself on the Mount as a hermit, hoping that others would come to join him in his eremitical lifestyle. They would be called the 'Hermits of the Sacred Heart of Jesus.' For this he would need to be a priest. At first he thought of being ordained in the Holy Land, but then thought that it would be better if he returned to France for his ordination.

Abbé Huvelin tried in vain to get Charles to abandon his plan of founding a congregation on the Mount, and to remain fast at Nazareth, at the convent of the Poor Clares. The Abbé knew Charles; he knew that, despite his personal holiness, he would not make a good founder of a religious community; he was too demanding on himself and he would have made the same demands on others.

Charles however, had already put his plans into action. He borrowed the necessary money to buy the Mount from his brother-in-law - 13,000 francs - but it seemed at the time that he was swindled by the sales agent, who had taken off with the money. Charles accepted this upset philosophically. He retained his plan to go to France to be ordained. God's wisdom is greater than human folly; as it turned out, events would arrange themselves both for Charles, who ended up going to Algeria, and for the Mount of Beatitudes which is, today, a Christian place of pilgrimage.

Charles returned to his first monastery, Our Lady of the Snows, and spent the winter and spring of 1900-01 studying theology and learning the ceremonies of the Mass. Dom Martin, the Abbot of Our Lady of the Snows, arranged that Charles should be accepted as a priest of the diocese of Viviers. Charles and the Abbott travelled to Viviers on the morning of June 9th 1901. Charles received the order of priesthood. He spent the night in adoration of the Holy Sacrament and on the morning of June 10th he offered his first Mass at Our Lady of the Snows. The chasuble he wore for the occasion had been made for him by Marie de Bondy. His sister, Mimi, received Holy Communion from his hand and having offered his thanksgiving he spent a long time with her.

While Charles was in France, he naturally reflected on where he was going to go once he had been ordained. As he later wrote: 'This life of Nazareth...was to be led elsewhere than in the Holy Land... This divine banquet whose minister I was to become, had to be offered... to the lame, blind and poor, to people, that is, without a priest... In Morocco... with ten million inhabitants, there was not a single priest.' It was natural that Charles' thoughts turned to Morocco, which he had come to love through his journey of exploration sixteen years earlier. In fact, once again events weren't to turn out as Charles would have liked: Morocco was to prove impossible to enter. However, Charles' plan was now clear: to go to live among the Muslims, not as a missionary in the normal sense, but to prepare the ground by his example for missionaries who would come after him.

Concretely, Charles (or Father de Foucauld, as he now was) wanted to set up a fraternity for adoration and hospitality. To achieve this, he proposed to act as chaplain to a remote military outpost; gaining the accord of the ecclesiastical, civil and military authorities in Algeria at the time, was no easy matter. Finally, he decided to go and plead his cause in person. He set sail for Algiers on September 6th, 1901.

Charles de Foucauld at Beni-Abbés.

ALGERIA: BENI ABBÉS

When he arrived he stayed, firstly with the White Fathers, and then with the Trappists at Staouëli. The Superior-General of the White Fathers, Monseigneur Livinhac was reluctant to allow this lone eccentric, with a rule that looked like folly, enter his territory: some of the tenets of Charles' rule for his new congregation were: Eagerness to shed a martyr's blood...Willingness to starve to death if necessary... Absolute obedience to Fr. de Foucauld, 'despite his unworthiness.' However, Charles eventually managed to get the necessary authorisation thanks to an old military friend, Major Henri Lacroix. And so he proceeded to establish himself at Beni Abbés, a garrisoned oasis near the border.

At Beni Abbés Charles bought fifteen acres of desert and built a small chapel. The altar was a gift from the monks of Our Lady of the Snows. He made a lining for the tabernacle from the chasuble he had used at his first Mass. Above the altar he placed a picture he had painted of Christ opening his arms to embrace humanity. Charles said: I want all the inhabitants, Christians, Muslim, Jew and idolater to regard me as their brother.

The oasis of Beni Abbés had a population of 1,200 to 1,300 people, not including the French troops. Charles started by buying some of the slaves who worked in the area and then liberating them, thereby causing annoyance to the French authorities. He also wrote to his friend, De Castries, and begged him to campaign in France for the abolition of slavery in French colonies. He was truly appalled at the misery of the slaves in Algeria. Their lives were blighted by daily beatings and gross overwork. If they tried to escape they were shot in the legs. And they were desperately undernourished. Charles provided a clinic for them. There he washed their ragged clothes for them, providing them with as much food as he could share and tried to heal their inner hurts.

Charles also tried to bring the soldiers back to the practice of their religious duties. Most of them had abandoned their Faith at least externally. He helped and encouraged them in every way possible. To a soldier who was suffering from depression he sent his most sympathetic invitation: "Dear friend, you told me that you were sad in the evenings... if you are allowed to leave the camp which I don't know, would you care to come habitually and spend the evenings with me: we will prolong them as long as is agreeable to you, talking in brotherly fashion about the future of your children, of your projects of what you desire and hope, for yourself and for those whom you love more than yourself... to make up for anything else, you will find here a brother's heart.

"You said you wanted a little history of St Paul... I would very much like to have written this for you but I can't, I have other urgent things to write at this moment... but I could tell it to you, interspersing my wretched words with passages from his letters, which I have got here and which are admirable... this poor man offers you what he has. What he offers you above all is his very tender, very brotherly affection and his profound devotion in the Heart of Jesus".

Universal brotherhood was already clearly more than a mere aspiration for Charles. October 21st 1901 was a day of great joy for Charles. From then on he said Sunday Mass at whatever time the soldiers could most easily attend. Generally he said his daily Mass shortly after 4 a.m. He had breakfast at 6 am, and this was followed by a Holy Hour. He spent the morning at work or at study. He spent some of the afternoon in adoration but he was also available for what he called 'necessary conversations'. In the evening he had a light meal and then he explained the gospels to any soldiers who cared to come. This Bible study was followed by a friendly chat. He retired shortly after eight but arose at midnight for Matins. During a typical day he had up to 100 visits. It was a demanding schedule.

One may wonder if Charles' presence and service to the people of Beni Abbés and later of Tamanrasset and Asekrem was impeded by his French nationality and his association with the French garrison. It would have to be borne in mind, however, that the people of Mediterranean Africa were not accustomed to either liberty or peace.

The area had long been a battle ground for French, Turks, Spanish and Portuguese. When invaders were not bothering the tribes they fought among themselves. There were rivalries between the Arabs and the Berbers, between the nomadic and the settled. It would appear that for a time at least the tribes in the oases were glad to have the comparatively stable regime brought by the French garrison. But it was also easy for rival powers to cause friction between the French and the native Arabic and Berber peoples.

In July 1903 fighting broke out between the Berber tribesmen and the French garrison. The Berber troops greatly outnumbered the garrison which was made up of French officers and native Algerian soldiers. Forty-nine men wounded in the fighting were moved to Taghit, a town one hundred and twenty kilometres from Beni Abbés. Charles pleaded to be allowed to go and minister to the wounded men and his request was granted. He was given a horse and, removing the Blessed Sacrament from the tabernacle, he set out. He covered the distance in twenty-four hours. Breaking down resistance by his kindness, he heard the confessions of the men and gave then Holy Communion. It was one of the few notable successes Charles had in his missionary labours.

Deeper in the desert

At around this time, Charles came under the influence of another old military acquaintance, the Commander-in-

SKETCH MAP OF ALGERIA

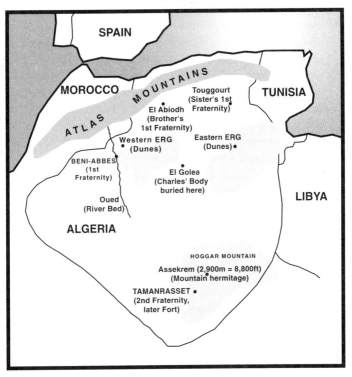

Map tracing the journey of Charles de Foucauld.

Chief of the southern Sahara, Henri Lapperine. Lapperine suggested to Charles that he go further south to be among the nomadic Saharan tribe, the Tuareg. Charles realised the impossibility of ever gaining access to Morocco. After some hesitation, but with the Abbé Huvelin's accord, Charles left Beni Abbés in January 1904. He travelled first to Adrar, then met up with Colonel Lapperine and the two of them covered three thousand miles and visited three hundred villages in the Southern Sahara. They were prevented from reaching Timbuktu by the French Niger Army which felt that Lapperine was encroaching on its territory. In September their return journey brought them to Ain Salah.

Charles had occupied much of his time during his travels with Lapperine and others in studying Tamahaqq, the language of the Tuaregs. It was spoken by members of the tribe in Algeria and Morocco. The script in which it was written was called Tifinagh.

The Tuaregs are a tall fair-skinned people. Their dress differs from that of other tribes in the Sahara in that it is not the women but the men who wear veils. The males wear a blue veil called a 'litham'. Before going to settle in the Ahaggar Charles spent six weeks with his religious superior, Monsignor Guerin, at Ghardaia. In January 1905 he returned to Beni Abbés. General Lyautey attended his Mass there and wrote of it: 'I've never heard Mass said as Father de Foucauld said it, it was one of the greatest impressions of my life".

The Mass was served by Paul Embarek, a slave liberated by Charles. He was not very reliable but his ability to serve Mass was valuable to the priest. Being a catechumen Paul was not allowed to receive Holy Communion.

Accompanied by a Captain Dinaux, Charles returned to the Sahara the following year. He visited a Tuareg Amenokal (Chief) called Moussa. The Captain introduced Charles as a Christian marabout (holy man) who served the one God, was devoted to solitude and anxious to continue his study of the Tamahaqq language. He would be of service to the ordinary inhabitants and would serve as a counsellor for Moussa himself.

Charles decided to build a hermitage in Tamanrasset, a settlement where there were cultivated lands and which was frequently visited by caravans. There was sufficient water there at least in winter. The serf class who tilled the land were called the Harratin. Above them in the social scale were the Imrad and the nobles with their Amenokal, Moussa.

Charles describes Moussa as 'Very intelligent, very frank, a very pious muslim but ambitious and fond of money, pleasure and honour'. Charles learned to love the people but viewed them at first with a certain suspicion, he wrote: "They have a violent character and violent habits that only force can control... they simply call us pagans and consider us as savages... they think themselves the most perfect people in the world... they are convinced Muslims but without knowledge and without practice of their religion."

Tamanrasset is now a town of nearly forty thousand people. When Charles went there it was a village of a mere twenty houses. The plateau of Tamanrasset is over four thousand feet above sea level. Despite its elevation extremely high temperatures are recorded there. The surrounding mountains are dazzlingly beautiful. On September 7th 1905, Charles celebrated Mass - the first Mass ever offered in Tamanrasset. In his relations with Moussa, Charles was greatly assisted by a beautiful woman called Dassine. Moussa hoped that some day he might conquer her heart and consequently she exercised great influence over him. Dassine was in the habit of holding tea-parties. Almost all the guests were women but sometimes Charles went along. He gave the women presents of sugar and needles. He, in turn, had an opportunity to improve his Tamahaqq.

Brother Michel

In November 1906 Charles visited the White Fathers at Maison Carée. A French student there was so impressed by Charles and his unique mission that he asked permission to join him. The permission was granted and together they proceeded to Beni Abbés where they spent Christmas. The young Breton, Brother Michel, has left a description of the Christmas Mass:

"About a hundred present, all French except for one old native woman (Marie) completely blind, who had been baptised by Father de Foucauld and who spent all her days in prayer and communicated every time Mass was said at Beni Abbés."

Christmas was, of course, for Charles and Michel a purely religious festival. There was no feasting. The typical midday meal was described by Michel: "then we would all sit down on our mats, around the saucepan, placed on the ground just as it came off the fire, the Father, our servant and I. We ate in the strictest silence, fishing out the food with a spoon, and drinking water from the same goblet. There was no variety in the menu; sometimes it was a dish of rice boiled in water, and exceptionally there was a little condensed milk with those carrots and turnips which grew in the sands of the desert, or else a sort of mixture of quite an agreeable taste, made with wheatmeal, crushed dates and water. No table napkins, no glasses, no tablecloth, no plates, no knives, no forks, to take this light collation."

Frère Michel did not reach Tamanrasset. He became ill on the journey and it was obvious that the demanding routine of Charles did not suit him. One recalls a comment made about Charles by the Abbot of Our Lady of the Snows. He wrote: "I must confess that I have some doubts about his prudence and discretion. The austerities which he practices and which he thinks he can impose on

his companions are of such a nature that I feel obliged to
believe that the beginner would succumb quite quickly".

The young Breton returned to France. He later became a
Carthusian. Strict as this order is it was not as demanding
as the routine Charles had imposed on the young monk.

Charles returned to Tamanrasset where he resumed
his life of service to his Tuareg neighbours. Using what
little medical skill he had, he passed on to them remedies
for their common ailments. He obtained these medica-
tions from friends in France. His friend Colonel
Lapperine saw to it that medical officers on their desert
rounds visited Tamanrasset.

One such welcome visitor was a Protestant doctor,
Claude Hérisson. He was deeply impressed by the hermit's humility and refinement. He saw that beneath
Charles' unimpressive appearance there was a lively per-
sonality, singular intelligence and a very kind compas-
sionate heart. "I saw", he wrote, "that he was idolised by
all the Frenchmen who already knew him".

Around this time Charles' servant Paul Embarek left
him. Charles now had nobody to serve at Mass and consequently he could not offer the Holy Sacrifice at all since
it was not permitted to celebrate mass alone. He was not
even allowed to keep the reserved host. But he chose to
sacrifice these things for a time, precious as they were to
him, to remain with the Tuareg. In the event, someone
interceded for him at Rome and Pope Pius X granted him

permission to say Mass alone so Charles could write in his diary on January 21st 1908: "Tomorrow I will be able to say Mass. Noel! Noel! Thank you, my God."

Charles of course could not share his Mass with the Tuaregs. They had only a minimal interest even in their own faith. But he made rosaries for them, teaching them to say on the small beads, "My God, I love You" and on the large beads "My God, I love You above all things."

Illness

It was at this time that Charles became seriously ill. There was a famine in the Ahaggar during the summer and autumn of 1907. Charles' ascetic lifestyle and over-work finally took its toll. He wrote to Lapperine and Bishop Guérin for 'a bit of milk and wine.' But a response to these requests was to take time.

Near death, it was the Tuareg people who came to Charles' aid. Moussa heard of Charles' illness and quickly did what he could for Charles, as did Dassine. They could not let the stranger among them die alone. This was a turning point in Charles' relationship with the Tuareg. For once they were responsible for him instead of it being always he who was giving to them. In the midst of famine, the Tuareg shared the little they had and saved Charles' life. From them on, Charles' relationship with the Tuareg was on a more equal footing.

The Tuareg Dictionary

Charles' illness interrupted his linguistic work, but when he had recovered, he resumed it. His friend, Colonel Laperrine described Charles at work:

'It is a godsend for him when he can get hold of a few elderly ladies of the Tuareg nobility, for it is they who are the most well versed in the tribal traditions. On those occasions, there is nothing more entertaining than to watch him holding court, pencil in hand, in the middle of an elite assembly of old dowagers sitting on the ground, chatting about everything while sipping their tea and smoking a pipe.'

Charles had received considerable help from an army officer and Arabic scholar, Captain Motylinski. The early death of the Captain deeply disturbed Charles. He very generously acknowledged his debt to Motylinski by publishing the Grammar and dictionary under Motylinski's name. He was also instrumental in having a fort named after his friend.

Charles' importance to the French military authorities was considerable. They appreciated his influence with the Tuareg people especially the middle class or 'Imrad'. But Charles was not an uncritical admirer of the military. Though he favoured French colonialism he could be quite critical of the vices of the colonisers. He once left Tamanrasset for two days to avoid welcoming an officer who had been cruel in his conduct towards the Tuaregs.

Despite his poverty by French standards, Charles was wealthy in the eyes of the indigenous inhabitants. His allowance from his family of twenty-five francs a month enabled him to buy small gifts as well as medicines for his neighbours. When, in 1917 and 1918, famine ravaged his people Moussa wrote touchingly: "Had the marabout (holy man) been alive they would not have died of hunger". Moussa had great reverence for Charles but he did not see any reason to follow Charles into the Catholic Church. His admiration for the marabout was tinged with pity. He once said of Charles "How is it, marabout, that you stay Christian? Don't you realise that as long as you do, your mortifications can be of no use to you?" But Moussa's conviction of the superiority of his own creed did not lessen his alliance with the French. When his friendship with Charles cooled slightly he remained loyal to the French powers.

Charles' idea for a Congregation

In December 1908 Charles made his first visit to France since his ordination and voluntary exile. He wished to discuss with Abbé Huvelin his plans for an association of lay people, and to get the necessary permission from the Church authorities. Despite a rebuff from the Archbishop of Paris, who bluntly told him to rejoin the Cistercians, Charles eventually succeeded in establishing a 'Union of Brothers and Sisters of the Sacred heart.' This was basically a group for lay people, but also included priests, nuns and monks. The 'Directory' which Charles wrote describing how such a group would live and be organized, includes sections on imitating Jesus, poverty, prayer, penitence and on 'the special duties of the brothers and sisters for the evangelization of the 'infidels' in their own country and in far-off countries.' This deep concern of Charles would certainly have been expressed differently today.

Return to Tamanrasset

His return to Tamanrasset was followed within a year by the deaths of three of Charles' closest friends. His religious superior Monsignor Guerin of the White Fathers and his college friend the Duc de Vallombrosa died in the same year. Vallombrosa was murdered in the Sahara by men of his own escort party. "One feels more and more alone in the world", commented Charles, but he added an affirmation of the consoling power of the abiding love of Jesus.

This abiding love of Jesus enabled him to go even deeper into the wilderness and to establish another hermitage at Asekrem, a mountainous place three days journey from Tamanrasset. In doing so he was following the people. Tamanrasset was practically deserted in summer when the inhabitants and their flocks moved up the mountain in search of fresh pastures. Asekrem was bitterly cold, with a daytime temperature of below zero. The winds howled around his hut. But the view from the door was breathtaking. He was frequently lost in admiration at the sight of the mountain peaks which surrounded him. "How good it is", he wrote, "to be in this great calm, surrounded by the beauties of nature, so tormented and so strange, and then to lift one's heart towards the Creator and Jesus the Saviour".

The solitude was tempered by visits from the families in the surrounding valleys. He shared his food with them and sometimes a group of people would spend a whole day with him. By this time Charles had his Tamahaqq Grammar and Dictionary and his collection of Tuareg poems and proverbs almost finished. The Tamahaqq - French dictionary runs to 2,028 pages in four volumes. The Tuareg poems, finished four days before his death runs to 1,119 pages in two volumes. The indebtedness of the Tuareg people to him was therefore not confined to the example of his holy life or to his gifts of food and medicine. Scholars and later Tuaregs have been enriched by Charles' linguistic work.

Charles had paid a second visit to France in 1911. His third visit, in 1913, was in part inspired by a desire to familiarise a representative Tuareg youth with French civilisation and French Catholicism. This young man, Ouksem, was homesick at times in the strange new country in which he found himself. Otherwise he would appear to have enjoyed his tour, acquiring incidentally, the skills of cycling and knitting. The knitting was, from a Tamanrasset viewpoint, the more practical of the two and Ouksem is reported to have passed on this skill to some Tuareg women. But his affection for French Catholicism and civilisation did not develop to any appreciable extent. A gun he obtained during his French tour was later used by him against the French in the Sahara.

During his sojourn in France, Charles abandoned his penitential diet and ate whatever was put before him. He also surprised his relatives by his reluctance to go to Vespers one Sunday evening. Perhaps he had already recited the office privately or perhaps he was just not in good form.

World War: the fort at Tamanrasset

Shortly after his return to the Sahara the world went to war. A campaign against French rule in the Sahara had begun several years earlier. This involved a Muslim sect called the Senoussis who allied themselves with the Turks. The Senoussis were violently anti-Christian and their Turkish and German support encouraged them to attack French outposts. Amongst their targets was the Christian 'marabout' at Tamanrasset.

Towards the end of 1915 Charles decided to build a fort, a solid structure of mud bricks, built under his directions by the local people in the village. The idea was to provide a safe refuge for the population of Tamanrasset, who were increasingly threatened by raiders from Morocco and from Tripolitania (now Southern Libya). The situation was exacerbated by the war in Europe between the colonial powers, and bands of Senoussi from the East were determined to expel the Europeans, then at their weakest, and establish Islamic rule. In early 1916 Charles, pressed by his Tuareg friends, moved into the fort with all his possessions, - his tabernacle and altar, his few books and his many pages of writings on the Tuareg language and culture. The fort contained provisions, and arms were provided at his request: thirty old rifles and six cases of ammunition, from the nearest French post.

According to a certain Captain Dupommier, writing a few months after Charles' death, "Fr de Foucauld resolutely refused to leave for the safety of the French fort at Motylinski (some 150 miles away)... He loved the poor people among whom he had lived for ten years, and did not want to abandon them at a time of danger, thinking he could be of use to them. He wanted to protect them, and it was for this purpose alone that... he asked for arms and built a little fort... to serve as a refuge and help repel marauders." The intention of Charles is clear, and needs to be seen in context with the times. Did Charles take the right means to the end he had in view? Opinions have and no doubt will continue to differ.

The last days

The fateful day was December 1st 1916. Charles had almost completed his daily routine of prayer and work. Letters he had written that day were found after his death. In one of these addressed to his cousin Marie de Bondy he had written: "Our annihilation is the most powerful means we have to unite ourselves to Jesus. One finds one doesn't love enough, - that's true; one will never love enough."

The mixed band of Senoussis, local Tuaregs and an African named El Madani whom Charles had befriended moved quietly in the direction of the fort. Their plan may have been to take Charles as a hostage. El Madani knocked at the door.

"Who is there?" Charles called from inside.

"It's the post from Motylinski", El Madani replied.

Charles opened the door and held out his hand to take the letters. Two Tuaregs grabbed him by the arms and pulled him across the threshold. His arms were bound behind his back and he was put sitting against the wall near the door. His servant Paul Embarek was placed to the left of the door and the raiders began to ravage the fort. Then two soldiers of the French Army, oblivious of the danger they were riding into, were seen approaching the fort. Charles made a movement, perhaps as a warning to the soldiers. Shots rang out. One of the soldiers fell dead. The other, who had only been wounded, was speedily dispatched. The Tuareg youth who was guarding Charles put his rifle to the priest's ear and shot him through the head. He died instantly. His body was stripped and thrown into the ditch which surrounded the fort. Paul Embarek was not harmed and he survived to give an eye-witness account of the shooting of Charles and the pillaging of the fort.

A small monstrance containing the Host was later found in the sand by a French officer. This officer had previously been told by Charles what to do with the Host in the event of the priest's death. Consequently, he carried the Host to Fort Motylinski. There a sergeant, who had once been a seminarian and who had remained a Catholic gave himself the Host in Holy Communion. Charles' body which had been crudely buried was exhumed the following year by his friend Laperrine who placed a plain wooden cross over the grave. In 1920 Laperrine himself died as a result of a plane crash. He was buried beside Charles. Charles' body was later transferred to El Golea where his tomb could be supervised by the White Fathers. His heart was appropriately retained in Tamanrasset. What Charles had written years ago in Nazareth proved prophetically true: "Think that you ought to die a martyr, stripped of everything, stretched naked on the ground and unrecognisable, covered with wounds and blood, killed violently and painfully -desire that it be today."

On December 13th Moussa, who at the time of the assasination was away from Ahaggar, wrote a letter to Charles' sister Marie, which was translated into French: "When I heard of the death of our friend, your brother Charles, my eyes closed. There was darkness all about me. I wept and shed tears." He ended, "Charles the marabout has died not only for all of you, he has died for us too. May God have mercy on him and may we meet him in Paradise."

Prayer

Father, I abandon myself into your hands;
Do with me what you will.
Whatever you may do, I thank you;
I am ready for all, I accept all.
Let only your will be done in me and in all your
creatures. I wish no more than this, O Lord.
Into your hands I commend my soul:
I offer it to you with all the love of my heart, for I love you, Lord, and so need to give myself, to surrender myself into your hands without reserve and with boundless confidence, for you are my Father.
(Prayer of Abandonment by Charles de Foucauld)

SOME WRITINGS OF BROTHER CHARLES

For the sake of Jesus and the Gospel

You ask me if I am ready to go somewhere else besides Beni Abbés to spread the Holy Gospel; for that, I am ready to go to the end of the world and to live till the last judgement. *(from a letter to a friend)*

We must read and re-read the Gospel without stopping, so that we will have the spirit, deeds, words, and thoughts of Jesus always before us and so that we may one day think, talk, and act as he did.
(from his personal notes)

The young agnostic

I was growing farther away, farther from you, my Lord and my life. And at the same time my life was becoming a living death; and in that dead state, still you were taking care of me. Yet how closely you were keeping me under your wings, even while I didn't even believe you existed!
(from his meditations)

Islam really shook me to the core. The sight of such faith, of these people living in the continual presence of

God, made me glimpse something greater, truer, than worldly concerns. I started studying Islam, and then the Bible. *(from a letter)*

But let us have hope! Because whatever our faults may be, Jesus wants to save us. The more we have sinned, the closer we are to death, the more desperate our situation, the more, so to speak, Jesus wants to save us, because he came to save what was being lost. *(from his meditations)*

The prodigal son was received not only with inexpressible goodness, without punishment, without reprimand, with no memories of the past, but was received with kisses, with the best tunic and the ring reserved for the son of the master of the house. Yes, he was was not only received like that, but was actually sought out by this blessed father, and carried back by him from the far-off country. *(from his meditations)*

Vocation: 'as Jesus of Nazareth'

The Incarnation has its source in the goodness of God. There is one thing that stands out as so wonderful, so astonishing, that it shines like a dazzling sign: the infinite humility contained in such a mystery. God, pure being, infinite, perfect, the Creator and sovereign Master of all, becomes a human being, uniting himself to a human soul and body, and appears on earth as a man, as the least of all people.

Like him, I should always seek out the very lowest place, to be as lowly as my Master, to walk behind him, step by step, as a faithful disciple.

See in this Incarnation such love for humanity, the love God has for us human beings, and consequently the love which you must have for each and every person in order to be like him, to be perfect as your heavenly Father is perfect.

In order to save us, God came close to us, mixed with us, lived with us in closest familiarity, from the Annunciation to the Ascension. For our salvation, he continues to come to us, to mix with us, to live with us in the closest possible contact, every moment of every day, in the Holy Eucharist. That is your model: in everything be like Jesus of Nazareth. *(from his meditations)*

Your Rule

Your rule: to follow me. To do what I would do. Ask yourself in everything: 'What would our Lord have done?', and do it. That is the only rule you have, but it is an absolute rule. *(from his meditations)*

As everyone knows, love demands imitation. It is impossible for me to understand how people can love and not want to share all Jesus' sorrows, not ardently desire to pattern their life on his. *(from a letter)*

Pray for me above all that I may have that burning, generous, passionate love that makes one love Jesus above all things. I don't ask to feel that love, nor to feel that Jesus loves me, as long as I love him with all my soul, passionately and for ever. *(from his meditations)*

Poor like Jesus

My Lord Jesus, how quickly those who love you with all their heart will become poor, for they couldn't endure being richer than their Beloved. To be rich, to live in comfort among my possessions, while you were poor, deprived, living as a workman under the burden of heavy labour, I just could not do it, my God: I could not love like that. *(from his meditations)*

Jesus was poor, and shared the life of the poor: I should do the same. *(from a letter)*

I don't believe there is any other line from the Gospel which has made a deeper impression on me or transformed my life as much as this one: 'Whatever you do to one of these little ones, you do to me.' If we think that these words were spoken by uncreated Truth, by the same lips which said, 'This is my body... this is my blood,' how forcefully we are driven back to seek out and love Jesus in these little ones, the sinners, the poor. *(from a letter)*

Your way of praying

Let us be persons of desire and of prayer. Let us never believe anything to be impossible: God can do all. *(from his meditations)*

We should read the Gospel with love, as though we were sitting at the feet of Jesus, at the feet of the Beloved, listening to him speak to us. *(from a letter)*

Prayer is just conversation with God: listening to him, speaking with him, gazing upon him in silence. The best prayer is the one in which there is the most love. *(from his meditations)*

Adoration, wordless admiration, that is the most eloquent form of prayer: that wordless admiration which contains the most passionate declaration of love. *(from his meditations)*

Our whole existence, our whole being has to proclaim the Gospel from the rooftops. Our whole person has to 'breathe' Jesus. All our actions, our whole life has to cry out that we belong to Jesus, we have to present the image of a life lived according to the Gospel. Our whole being has to be a living proclamation, a reflection of Jesus, has to 'breathe' his beauty, make him visible, be a shining image of Jesus. *(from his meditations)*

Your relationship with others

See Jesus in every human being, and act on that vision:
with goodness, respect, love, humility, gentleness... Live
for Jesus, more than for myself. *(from his meditations)*

I want all the people here, Christians, Muslims, Jews, non-
believers, to get used to seeing me as their brother, the brother
of all. They have started calling my place 'the Fraternity', and
I am really pleased about that. *(from a letter)*

[Jesus speaks:] 'It is love which should help you to be
recollected in me, and not remaining distant from my
children. See me in them, and just as I did in Nazareth,
live close to them, lost in God'. *(from his diary, 1904)*

It is good to live alone here (in Tamanrasset), you accom-
plish something even without doing much of anything,
because you become more and more one of the local people. You are so ordinary and approachable. *(from a letter)*

I have chosen Tamanrasset, in the heart of the Hoggar, in
the midst of the Dag Rali, the principal Tuareg tribe. Here,
in the very centre of the Sahara, is I think where the
Beloved wants me to be, in this village of twenty homes
deep in the mountains. I chose this abandoned spot and I
have settled here, begging Jesus to bless this foundation

where I want his Nazareth life to be the only model for
my own.

I divide my time between prayer, contacts with the
local people, and work on the Tuareg language. I put a lot
of time into this last: the only way I can do any good for
the Tuareg is talking with them, and learning their language is indispensable. Besides, it has its own value.

My apostolate is simply 'goodness': seeing me, others
should say, 'If this man aims at being good, his religion
must be good'. And if anyone asks me why I try to be
gentle and good, I have to say, 'Because I am the servant
of someone so much better than me: if only you knew
how good Jesus my Master is!'

The Tuareg in this area trust me more and more: old
friendships are growing deeper, new friendships are
forming. I do them whatever services I can, I try to show
them my love. When the occasion arises, I speak with
them about natural religion, the commandments of God,
God's Love, union with his will, love of neighbour...

It's good to become all things to all people in order to
bring them all to Jesus - having for every person the
goodness and affection of a brother or a sister: doing
whatever service we can and striking up friendly relations; being a caring brother or sister to everyone so as to
bring people little by little to Jesus, by practising the kind
of gentleness he practised... *(from various letters)*

'All things to all people'

All Christians have to be apostles. That is not a counsel, it is a commandment of love. Lay people should all be apostles towards everybody they can reach: those that are their friends first, but not only them. Love has nothing narrow about it. It takes in all those whom the heart of Jesus embraces.

One should try to become 'all things to all people', in order to bring them to Jesus - having for every person the goodness and affection of a brother or sister; doing whatever service we can, striking up friendly relations; being a caring brother or sister to everyone in order to lead people little by little to Jesus, by practicing the kind of gentleness he practiced. *(from a letter)*

Preparing for death

You tell me, Lord, that I will be happy, with the truest kind of happiness, on the last day. That, worthless as I am, I am a palm tree beside the flowing waters of God's will, of God's love, of grace - and that I will bear my fruit in due season. *(from his meditations)*

When the grain of wheat that falls into the ground does not die, it remains alone; if it dies it bears much fruit. I have not died, and so I am alone. Pray for my conversion, so that I may die, and bear fruit. *(from a letter)*

Think that you must die as a martyr, stripped of everything, stretched out on the ground, naked, unrecognisable, violently and painfully killed... and want it to be today. *(from his meditations)*

Whatever their reasons for killing us, if we, interiorly, receive an unjust and cruel death as a blessed gift of your hand, if we thank you for it as we would for a welcome grace, as a happy imitation of the way you met death, if we offer it to you as a free and willing sacrifice, if we put up no resistance in order to obey your words 'Do not resist evil' and to follow your example: 'He was silent before his shearers and let himself be slaughtered without complaint' - then, whatever they might kill us for, we will die in pure love, and our death will be a most fragrant offering to you. And if it is not martyrdom in the strict sense of the word, as people see it, yet it will be so in your eyes, and it will be a most perfect image of your death. *(from his meditations)*

A final word

Thanks, my dear 'Mother', for your letters, just arrived this morning, as well as for the tin of cocoa: you are really spoiling your old 'son'!

I hope that when my reply reaches you in the new year, you will be in better form. I understand well your distress and anxiety. How could you not feel the weight of years and troubles? How could you not be worried by

the agonies of two years of war and by the constant concern for the safety of your son? Yes, such trials risk
crushing us. But these sufferings, which we cannot
escape, if accepted and offered to God in union with the
sufferings of Jesus are not the only thing, but the most
precious that the good God offers you so that you come
before him with full hands. Probably you feel empty-
handed and I am glad that you do so, but I have the firm
hope that the good Lord is not of your opinion: he has
given you too great a share in his 'chalice',which you
have faithfully accepted, for him not to give you a great
share in his glory. Our own 'annihilation' is the most
powerful means we have of uniting ourselves with Jesus
and doing good to people (it is what St. John of the Cross
says in one way or another on almost every page). When
we are able to suffer and to love, we are capable of much,
we can do the greatest thing it is possible to do in this
world. We feel when we suffer; we do not always feel
when we love - and that makes us suffer even more! But
we know that we would like to love, and to want to love
is to love. We find we do not love enough; how true! - we
will never love enough. But God knows what kind of clay
he fashioned us out of, and he loves us more than a mother could love her child. And he who does not lie has told
us that he would never reject anyone who came to him.
(*from a letter written on the day of his death*)

THE LEGACY OF BROTHER CHARLES

Charles desired to found both male and female congregations, and also to encourage lay people in France to be concerned with the disadvantaged, both in near and in far-off countries. During Charles' life-time, the one group which was created, in France, was the 'Union of Brothers and Sisters of the Sacred Heart.' This group of mostly lay people included 49 members at Charles' death. One of these members was Louis Massignon (1883-1962), a world-renowned scholar of Islam. Louis Massignon contacted a well-known French novelist, René Bazin, who agreed to write a biography of Charles. This work, (*Charles de Foucauld, explorer of Morocco, hermit of the Sahara*) appeared in 1921. The 'Union' continued to grow; today it consists of 4,000 members worldwide, in all five continents. It consists of groups of lay or religious members who meet regularly, to pray and to discuss their faith and lives. In England these groups consist of both Catholic and Anglican members.

The Little Brothers

It was Bazin's biography which first publicised de Foucauld's life, and sparked off the numerous groups and associations which have since developed. In 1933 René

Voillaume founded, with four companions, what was later to become the Little Brothers of Jesus. Originally, this was a monastic congregation, but it developed, in the 1950s into a congregation of small fraternities of 2-4 brothers who lived out their contemplative life-style by taking manual jobs within the community. One brother, for example was a fisherman off the coast of Brittany in France. Another worked in circuses which toured Europe; others worked alongside miners in Germany and Belgium. One brother worked in engineering and chemical factories in Leeds, Yorkshire.

The Little Sisters

In 1939 the Little Sisters of Jesus were founded by Magdeleine Hutin. From the very beginning, the Little Sisters lived their prayerful witness through an active participation in the local community taking low-paid jobs and founding their fraternities in a wide range of settings: for example, with the Pygmies in central Africa (since 1952); the Eskimos of Alaska (since 1954); the Aborigines of central Australia (since 1954). In Europe there are a number of travelling fraternities: in funfairs and circuses, and with the gypsies. In England and Ireland, as also in Europe, the Little Sisters continue to live their Nazareth life in inner cities. They are continually searching to be present to the new poverties of our age in whatever forms they take. Today there are about 1,200 sisters from 62 nationalities.

Other Groups

In 1951 a priests' fraternity was begun. This consists of groups of 8-12 priest who meet to discuss and pray together once a month. They are specially aware of the needs of the poor. Today there are 3,500 members worldwide.

There are many other members of the 'Charles de Foucauld family.' One is the Little Brothers and Sisters of the Gospel, who have a slightly more evangelical vocation than the Little Brothers and Sisters of Jesus; they will sometimes take parish work and are involved in social work to alleviate the condition of the poor in some countries. They began in 1956 in the Cameroons: some people, where they were living, came to the Little Brothers of Jesus asking to be baptised. The Little Brothers of Jesus felt that this was not part of their vocation... and thus, the Little Brothers and Sisters of the Gospel were born.

Various other groups of the last 40 years have taken the original ideas of Brother Charles concerning an authentic Christian witness as the basis of their foundations. One of these is a group of celibate lay women, the Fraternity of Charles de Foucauld, some members of which are in England.

The Future

What does the future of the groups founded by Br. Charles hold? Like all Christian groups they are faced by increasing secularisation, and by the decrease of the practice of faith in Western countries. Yet their emphasis on a Christian witness that speaks through its deeds, rather than by its preaching, is in tune with what many younger people are seeking today. By holding on to their vocation of being with and yet by also working for those who are excluded from society, the Charles de Foucauld family will continue to inspire Christians and non-Christians alike.

Bibliography

Charles de Foucauld's own writings (apart from his works on the Tuareg language and culture which were published, at his request, under another name) are mainly in the form of personal notes and meditations (intended only for his own use) and letters. Most of this is published in French. There are a number of biographies in both languages, but only a few in print. Below is a list of the most easily available books.

In French

Oeuvres spirituelles de Charles de Foucauld - 16 volumes (Nouvelle Cite 1974-1997).

Biographies by René Bazin, Michel Carrouges, M. Castillon du Perron, J.-F. Six.

In English

Books which may be in libraries:
Marion M. Preminger, *The Sands of Tamanrasset*, Hawthorn Books: USA, 1961.

Elizabeth Hamilton, *The Desert my Dwelling Place*, Hodder & Stoughton, 1968.

Books in print, available also through Amazon on the internet:
Michel Lafon, *15 Days of Prayer with Charles de Foucauld*, Liguori: Missouri, 1999.

Robert Ellsberg, *Charles de Foucauld: Selected Writings*, Orbis: Maryknoll, N.Y., 1999.

Jean-Jacques Antier, *Charles de Foucauld*, Ignatius Press: San Francisco, 1999.

Books on the Charles de Foucauld Family:
René Voillaume, the founder of the Little Brothers of Jesus has written many books, which are mostly out of print; his most celebrated book is *Seeds of the Desert*, (Anthony Clarke: Wheathampstead, 1972/85).

Carlo Carretto, a Little Brother of the Gospel has also written many books, such as *Letters from the Desert* (Darton, Longman and Todd: London, 1972/90).

On Little Sister Magdeleine:
Katherine Spink, *The Call of the Desert: A Biography of Little Sister Magdeleine of Jesus*, DLT: London, 1993.

Little Sister Magdeleine, *He took me by the hand: The Little Sisters of Jesus following in the footsteps of Charles de Foucauld*, New City: London, 1991.

There is also a video available: *Seeds of the Desert: The legacy of Charles de Foucauld*, available from 148 Fellows Court, London E2 8LW.

To Contact for Further Information

Lay Fraternities
Margaret Kerbey, 73 Woolton Road, Garston, Liverpool L19 5ND

Jesus-Caritas Priests' Fraternity
Fr Anthony Charlton, Priests' House, 25 Dunley Drive, New Addington, Surrey CR0 0RG

Little Brothers of Jesus
Br Ian Latham, 82 Cronin Street, London SE15 6JG

Little Sisters of Jesus
L S Deirdre, 18 Donard View, Bishop's Court, Downpatrick, Co Down, Northern Ireland BT 30 7BN (01396 - 841085) (UK) 148 Fellows Court, London E2 8LW

Fraternity of Charles de Foucauld
(lay women committed to celibacy)
Phyllis Smith, 19 Gerrards Close, Southgate London N14 4RH

Jesus Caritas Website: http://www.jc.gn.apc.org
Produced by Pam Ware, 34 Gateley Road, London SW9 9SZ